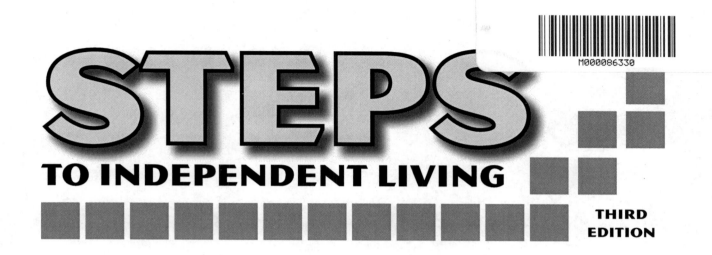

STEPS
TO INDEPENDENT LIVING

THIRD EDITION

How to Use Money Wisely

Nancy Lobb

illustrated by David Strauch

WALCH EDUCATION

SUSTAINABLE FORESTRY INITIATIVE

Certified Chain of Custody
Promoting Sustainable
Forest Management

www.sfiprogram.org

SGS-SFI/COC-US09/5501

1   2   3   4   5   6   7   8   9   10

ISBN 978-0-8251-6493-4

Contents

To the Student . . . . *v*

Self-Test . . . . *vi*

Part 1: Using Your Money Wisely

Check Out a Paycheck. 3

Plan Your Spending 5

Take Charge of Your Spending 9

A Spending Plan 10

Check Yourself 11

Part 2: Using the Bank

Why You Should Have a Bank Account 17

Choosing a Bank 18

Check Yourself 19

Opening a Checking Account 21

How a Checking Account Works 23

Writing Checks 24

Using a Debit, or ATM, Card 26

ATM Safety 28

Online Banking 29

Check Yourself 31

A Savings Account 34

Credit Cards. 37

Using a Credit Card. 39

A Bank Loan 41

Keeping Your Personal Information Safe 42

Check Yourself 44

Part 3: Being a Wise Consumer

Be a Careful Shopper 53

Comparison Shopping Is the Key 54

Think Before You Buy 55

Where to Buy 57

When to Buy 58

Saving Money at the Grocery Store or Drug Store 59

Be Advised 61

Read the Warranty. 63

Complain, Complain! 65

Check Yourself 67

Your Weekly Shopping 70

Brand Name or Store Brand? 72

Unit Pricing. 73

Check Yourself 74

Words to Know. 77

To the Student

Living on your own can be a great experience! You can choose and decorate your own place. You can decide for yourself what and when to eat. You can set your own hours. In short, you are free to make your own choices about your lifestyle.

Along with these freedoms comes responsibility. Living on your own means it's up to you to take care of yourself when you're sick or hurt. You are now the one who must be sure your nutritional, physical, and emotional needs are met. No one will be watching over you to ensure your personal safety. No one will be looking to make sure you make good decisions about alcohol, drugs, and tobacco. It's up to you!

But that's not all! You must make good choices as you choose and set up your home. You must keep your home safe and clean. And you must use your money wisely to meet your needs.

You will have a better experience living on your own if you are prepared to meet your new responsibilities. The six books in the *Steps to Independent Living* series will teach you the skills you need to make it on your own.

In this book, *How to Use Money Wisely,* you will learn about:

- making the most of your money
- using the bank
- being a wise consumer

We hope this information helps prepare you for the day you start living on your own!

www.walch.com

Self-Test

How much do you know about using money wisely? Circle YES or NO for each question.

1. Do you know how to plan your spending so you have money for things you really want?

    YES   NO

2. Do you know how to find out where your money goes each month?

    YES   NO

3. Do you know how to choose a bank that will meet your needs?

    YES   NO

4. Do you know how to open a savings or checking account?

    YES   NO

5. Do you know how to write checks?

    YES   NO

6. Do you know when it's a good idea to use your credit cards?

    YES   NO

7. Do you know how to keep your use of credit under control?

    YES   NO

8. Do you know how to take out a bank loan?

    YES   NO

9. Do you know how to get the most for your money when you buy big-ticket items?

    YES   NO

www.walch.com

10. Do you know how to save money on your weekly shopping trips?

    YES   NO

11. Do you know when is the best time to buy pillows, lawn mowers, and clothes?

    YES   NO

12. Do you know what to do if you buy an item that does not work or is spoiled?

    YES   NO

13. Do you know how to use online banking?

    YES   NO

14. Do you know how to use a debit card correctly?

    YES   NO

15. Do you know how to keep safe while using an ATM?

    YES   NO

16. Do you know how CDs and money market accounts work?

    YES   NO

17. Do you know how to avoid identity theft?

    YES   NO

How many YES answers did you have? _____

After you read this book, take the self-test again.

How many YES answers did you have this time? _____

PART 1

Using Your Money Wisely

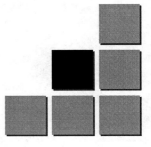

Check Out a Paycheck

One of the best things about working is getting paid! It's a good feeling to earn your own money. Look at the sample paycheck on the next page. Here are a few things you should know about a paycheck.

Gross Pay

Let's say you worked 40 hours one week, at $7 an hour. That means you earned $280 that week (40 hours × $7). The $280 is called your gross pay. But you will not get all $280.

Deductions

Certain amounts will be taken away (deducted) from your gross pay. There are deductions for federal income tax and state income tax. There is a deduction for FICA. FICA stands for the Federal Insurance Contributions Act. (FICA money goes into a government account known as Social Security.) There may be other deductions, too.

Net Pay

The deductions have been taken out. Is there anything left? Whatever is left is your take-home pay, or your net pay.

Sample Paycheck

<table>
<tr><td colspan="2">ABC Products
123 South Street
Chicago, IL 33489</td><td colspan="2">Name: Maria Lopez</td></tr>
<tr><td colspan="2"></td><td colspan="2">Date of check: July 31</td></tr>
<tr><td colspan="2">Gross Pay:</td><td colspan="2">$280</td></tr>
<tr><td colspan="2">Decuctions:</td><td colspan="2"></td></tr>
<tr><td colspan="2">Federal Withholding Tax</td><td colspan="2">$28</td></tr>
<tr><td colspan="2">State Withholding Tax</td><td colspan="2">$11</td></tr>
<tr><td colspan="2">FICA Tax</td><td colspan="2">$12</td></tr>
<tr><td colspan="2">Life Insurance</td><td colspan="2">$ 3</td></tr>
<tr><td colspan="2">Health Insurance</td><td colspan="2">$15</td></tr>
<tr><td colspan="2">Parking</td><td colspan="2">$ 5</td></tr>
<tr><td colspan="2">Credit Union</td><td colspan="2">$25</td></tr>
<tr><td colspan="2">Total Deductions:</td><td colspan="2">$99</td></tr>
<tr><td colspan="2"></td><td colspan="2"></td></tr>
<tr><td colspan="2">NET PAY:</td><td colspan="2">$181</td></tr>
</table>

ABC Products
123 South Street
Chicago, IL 33489

323

Date July 31, 2008

Pay to the order of: Maria Lopez

$181.00

One Hundred Eighty One and 00/100   Dollars

STANDARD BANK
P. O. BOX 300
WELLINGTON, NY 10232

⑆ 3333333333⑆ 600010477815

Plan Your Spending

Now you have your net pay in hand. Chances are that it's not as much as you'd like it to be. You have a limited amount of money to pay for all the things you need and want. The answer to this problem is to learn to use the money you have wisely.

Many people don't like the idea of planning their spending. They think it means doing without and not having any fun. They are wrong! By planning your spending, you are more likely to have the money to pay for things you really want or need.

There are six steps to planning your spending:

1. **The first step is to figure out how much money you can depend on earning every month.** First is your paycheck. You may also receive government payments or child support. You might have interest income. Add all your sources of income together. Include only those you are sure to get each month.

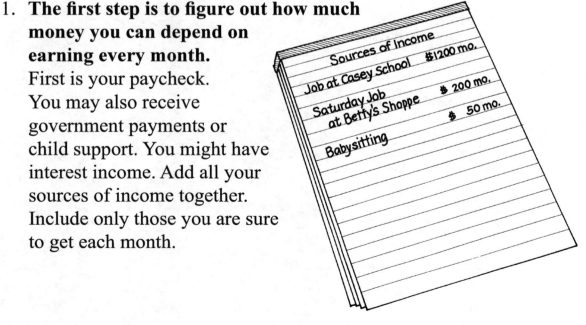

Sources of Income

Job at Casey School $1200 mo.

Saturday Job
at Betty's Shoppe $ 200 mo.

                              $ 50 mo.

Babysitting

2. **The second step in planning your spending is to plan to meet your basic needs. Needs** are the things you must have to live—not frills or extras. Food, clothing, and a place to live are some basic needs. You will have other fixed costs as well. These might include car payments, health insurance, and so forth. Other expenses such as entertainment are **wants.** You want them but do not have to have them in order to live.

What do you think are some basic needs for a young person living on her or his own in an apartment? (Do not include wants on your list.)

Below are a few suggestions. Beside each, estimate how much money you might need for that item.

   a. Rent (or mortgage) payment

   b. Utilities

   c. Car expenses

   d. Groceries

   e. Insurance

   f. Taxes

g. Savings

h. Other: _____

i. Other: _____

Total: _____

3. **The next step is to set goals for yourself.** Then you save your money to meet your goals. Goals are things you want to do. One person's goal might be saving for a trip. Someone else might save for new clothes. Another person may want to buy a car. Everyone's goals are different.

Needs
Job
Food
Rent
Healthcare
Car
Commute

Think about your own goals. Write them here. Put a check by each goal you are saving for now.

☐ _____

☐ _____

☐ _____

☐ _____

☐ _____

☐ _____

4. **The fourth step in planned spending is to think before you buy.** Most people have more wants and needs than money. So it's important to learn to get the most out of your dollars. A good way to do this is to learn to buy wisely. We'll talk more about this in Part 3 of this book.

5. **The fifth way to make your money go further is to take care of the things you already own.** If your things last longer, you save!

6. **The sixth spending hint is to avoid borrowing money.** Do you always have more monthly needs than money? Many people do. Borrowing is not always bad. But you must pay interest or consider paying back a loan when you borrow money. This often means that you will end up with less money the next month. It's best to try to live within your means!

www.walch.com

Take Charge of Your Spending

We have talked about setting goals. But how can you squeeze out money to save toward your goals?

You might win the lottery. Or you might marry someone who has a lot of money. But if you're like most of us, you'll have to save from what you earn.

To do this, you must get in control of your cash. Cash slips through your fingers every day, and you never notice it!

Here's how to find out where that slippery cash goes:

1. **Write down everything you spend.** Do it every day for a month. Don't forget anything. A candy bar, a soft drink, a magazine—record it all! At the end of the month, you will see where your money has gone.

2. **Look over the list.** Try to pick one or two things you could cut back on or cut out. That cash is then freed for savings.

3. **Pay yourself first.** Put the money you've saved in a savings account at the first of the month—and leave it there!

To get money for something you want, spend less on something else. That's all there is to it.

A Spending Plan

Now that you have decided to take charge of your money, you can make a spending plan. This is a way to prepare for where your money will go each month.

First, put your goal at the top of the plan. This is to remind you why you are making the plan to begin with. Put aside the money for your goal. Then juggle what is left to meet your other needs and wants.

Make a spending plan for yourself. Write your goal at the top. Then list your expenses and how much you plan to spend on each. At the end of the month, write how much you really spent.

Spending Plan

Month: _____

I am saving for this goal: _____

Expenses	I plan to spend this:	I really spent this:
1. Savings for goal		
2.		
3.		
4.		
5.		
6.		
7.		
8.		
9.		
Totals:		

Check Yourself

1. Name five common paycheck deductions.

   a.

   b.

   c.

   d.

   e.

2. What is another name for take-home pay?

3. What do you think is the most important reason to plan your spending?

Continued ➡

www.walch.com

4. Why do you think setting a goal should be an important step in planning your spending?

5. How do you think borrowing money can upset your spending plan?

6. List the three steps for getting control of what you spend.

   a.

   b.

   c.

7. How do you think making a spending plan could help you do a better job of managing your money?

Continued

8. What is gross pay?

9. How can taking care of things you already own help you make your money go further?

10. Why is it important to pay yourself first when trying to save money?

11. What is the first step in planning your spending?

12. What is FICA?

13. What is the difference between wants and needs?

14. Why do you think many people do not want to plan their spending?

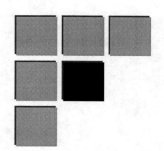

PART 2

Using the Bank

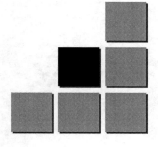

Why You Should
Have a Bank Account

Some people cash their paycheck and pay for everything in dollars. There's a better way: having a bank account. Here's why this is a better idea:

- If your money is in the bank, it is safe from theft or loss.

- A savings account can help you save money.

- You may get to know the bank manager over time. Then when you need other bank services in the future, you will feel comfortable asking for information.

- If you have a checking account, you won't need to buy cashier's checks or money orders to pay bills.

Choosing a Bank

There are many banks in most towns. How can you choose which one to do business with?

- Choose a bank that's close to where you live or work.

- Ask friends or family where they bank. Find out if they are happy with their bank's services.

- Check the bank's hours to be sure they will work for you.

- Find out where the bank's ATMs are located.

- Check whether the bank offers online banking services. It can be convenient to pay bills or check your account balances online.

- Ask what types of checking or savings accounts the bank offers.

- See what types of fees the bank charges for checking and savings accounts.

- See if you are a member of a group that has a credit union. Credit unions are often formed by groups of people who work together. Credit unions are non-profit. That means they may be able to offer you better deals than a regular bank.

- Make sure the bank is insured by the Federal Deposit Insurance Corporation (FDIC). That means your account is insured by the federal government.

Check Yourself

Write TRUE or FALSE on the line in front of each statement that follows. If the statement is false, explain why.

_____ 1. When choosing a bank, don't worry about its location.

_____ 2. All banks are open for the same hours.

_____ 3. Credit unions are open to everyone who wants to open an account.

_____ 4. A bank insured by the FDIC will offer lower rates on car loans.

www.walch.com

_____ 5. If you build a relationship with a bank, the bank will be more likely to loan you money in the future.

_____ 6. Money deposited in a bank insured by the FDIC is insured by the federal government against theft or loss.

_____ 7. By law, all banks must charge the same fees for checking accounts and ATMs.

_____ 8. Credit unions are non-profit groups.

www.walch.com

Opening a Checking Account

A checking account is a good way to keep track of your money. When you pay by check, you have a record of where your money has gone. Also, your money is safe in the bank.

You deposit money in a checking account. Then you can write checks to pay bills or for things you buy. You may also get a debit or ATM card that you can use to pay for purchases. The money is subtracted from your checking account. (We will talk more about these on pages 26–28).

When you're ready to open a checking account, go into the bank. There may be a desk marked "New Accounts." If not, any bank officer can help you.

Explain your banking needs to the bank officer. Ask the bank officer to explain the different types of accounts that would fit your needs.

Here are a few questions to ask when opening a new account:

- How much money will I need to open the account?

- Is there a minimum amount of money that must be kept in the account at all times?

- Does the account pay interest? If so, how much?

- Is there a charge for writing a check?

- Is there a limit to how many checks I can write each month without having to pay a fee?

- What is the charge for a bounced check?

- Can I use a debit card with this account? (Read more about this on pages 26–28.)

- Is there a charge for using the debit card at this bank?

- Is there a charge for using the debit card at another bank?

- Do you have online banking? (Read more about this on pages 29–30.)

Some banks offer free checking. Look for an account that has:

- unlimited monthly check writing

- free online access to your account

- free ATM or debit card

- free checks

- free online bill pay

- no charge to use ATMs of other banks

After opening an account, get a file folder and put the information about your new account into it. Label it with the bank's name and the type of account. Make a separate folder for each account you open. If you will be getting statements from the bank, you can put these in the folder when they come. That way all your paperwork will be organized.

How a Checking Account Works

When you open a checking account, you order a pad of checks. Be careful what personal information you put on your checks. Never put private forms of identification such as your Social Security number or driver's license number on your checks.

You may also get a debit card or ATM card when you open an account. Be sure you understand how these cards work before you use them. An ATM is an automated teller machine.

When you get your checks, you will also get a ledger to record how much money you spend or put in the account. Use the ledger to write down each check you write and deposit you make. Subtract the checks. Add the deposits. That way you know how much money you have in your account.

Once a month, you will get a bank statement. It is a record of the deposits, withdrawals, and balance on the account. Read the statement carefully. Learn to balance your checkbook. (A bank officer can show you how.) That way you'll catch any mistakes made by yourself or the bank. And you'll always know how much money you have in your account.

STANDARD BANK

Send inquiries to Standard Bank, P. O. Box 300, Wellington, NY 10232 (217) 450-3000

STATEMENT

John Johnson
135 Center St.
Wellington, NY 10236

Checking Acct. No. 7173300560
Statement Period: 05/01 - 05/31/10

			Balance
Previous Balance			$ 1,095.00
05/02	Draft 321	950.00	145.00
05/06	Direct Deposit	600.00	745.00
05/08	Draft 322	35.00	710.00
05/12	Draft 323	63.85	646.15
05/14	Draft 324	75.00	571.15
05/20	Direct Deposit	600.00	1171.15
05/20	ATM Withdrawal	100.00	1071.15
05/31	End of Month Balance		$ 1071.15

Writing Checks

Learn to write checks safely. When you fill in the dollar amount, make sure you write in a way that keeps someone from adding numbers to it. For example, if your check is for $20, put the 2 as far left as possible. Then draw a line after the 0 to the end of the space. That way there is no place for someone to write more numbers.

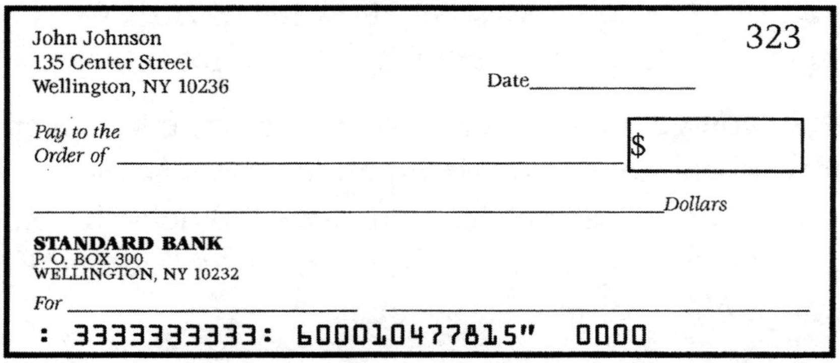
John Johnson
135 Center Street
Wellington, NY 10236
323
Date
Pay to the
Order of
$
Dollars
STANDARD BANK
P. O. BOX 300
WELLINGTON, NY 10232
For
: 3333333333: 600010477815" 0000

Always sign your checks the same way. Sign your checks in cursive. Never sign a blank check. Someone could fill it out for any amount of money they wanted. Of course, always use ink (never pencil) to write a check!

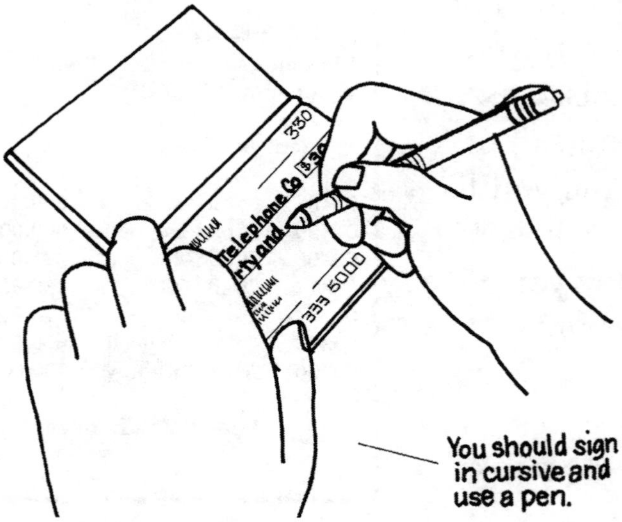
You should sign in cursive and use a pen.

Fill out the checks below. Use today's date. Use your own signature.

To BeBop Fashions for $32.50:

John Johnson
135 Center Street
Wellington, NY 10236

Date_____

323

Pay to the
Order of _____

$ _____

_____*Dollars*

STANDARD BANK
P. O. BOX 300
WELLINGTON, NY 10232

For _____   _____

⑆ 3333333333⑆ ⑈00010477815⑈ 0000

To Jones Auto Parts for $16.95:

John Johnson
135 Center Street
Wellington, NY 10236

Date_____

323

Pay to the
Order of _____

$ _____

_____*Dollars*

STANDARD BANK
P. O. BOX 300
WELLINGTON, NY 10232

For _____   _____

⑆ 3333333333⑆ ⑈00010477815⑈ 0000

Using a Debit, or ATM, Card

Debit cards are often known as ATM cards or check cards. Debit cards look like credit cards, but they work more like a personal check.

In fact, some people like to use a debit card instead of writing checks. They find that it is faster and easier. When you use a debit card, the money is subtracted out of your account right away. You cannot spend more money than you have in your checking account.

When you get a debit card, you choose a personal identification number (PIN) to go with it. Each time you use the card, the machine you are using will ask you to type in your PIN. This helps to keep other people from using your card.

Debit cards work in an ATM (automated teller machine). You can go to an ATM to get cash when you need it.

Debit cards also work in grocery stores, gas stations, restaurants, and stores at the mall. You use the card to pay for what you are buying.

It's important to keep track of purchases made with a debit card. Write these amounts in your checkbook right away so you don't forget them.

Debit cards are easier to get than a credit card. You may be given a debit card when you open a checking account.

Debit cards are good because you don't have to carry a lot of cash or a checkbook. You also cannot run into debt using a debit card. But, you can run out of money!

Be careful with your debit card. Remember, the money comes right out of your checking account. You may be charged a fee when you use your debit card.

Keep your debit card receipts. Keep track of your account balance. Be aware that some banks have a limit on how many times a day you can use your debit card.

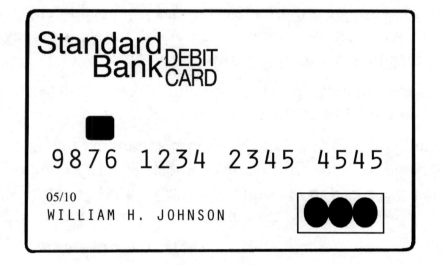

www.walch.com

ATM Safety

Be alert when you use an automated teller machine (ATM). Don't use the machine if someone nearby is making you uneasy. Choose an ATM that is well-lit and monitored by cameras.

Use an ATM quickly. When you get to an ATM, have your card ready. Use your free hand to cover the keyboard as you type in your personal identification number (PIN). The personal identification number is a private code that you need to enter to activate the ATM. Before you leave the ATM, put your money, card, and receipt away in your wallet.

Be sure you pick up the receipt after using the ATM. Leaving it at the ATM could cause you trouble later.

When you decide on a PIN, choose something that is not obvious. Never use your birth date or Social Security number. Never keep your PIN in the same place as your ATM card. Don't give anyone else your number.

If you lose your ATM or debit card, call the bank right away. They can put a hold on your account to make sure no one else can use your card.

www.walch.com

Online Banking

Online banking is also known as Internet banking. Online banking allows bank customers to manage their accounts on a secure Web site operated by their bank or credit union.

Different banks will have various services available online. Some banks charge a small fee. With other banks, the service is free. Check with your bank to find out. Larger banks are likely to offer these services:

- paying bills online

- transferring money between your checking and savings accounts

- checking the balance on your accounts

- checking your monthly bank statement

- seeing images and printing copies of checks you have written

Paying bills online can save you time and money. The bank's Web site will walk you through the steps for getting set up. You have to enter information about the bills you want to pay and which accounts you'll use to pay them. Once all this is set up, paying your bills online will be fast and easy.

You will have a user name and password to access your online account. There will be an icon (small picture) on the Web page (usually an icon of a locked padlock) to let you know the site is secure.

Some banks exist only on the Internet. There is no bank building to visit in town. These online banks may offer the same services as your local bank. They may pay higher interest and have lower fees. But they have no ATM machines. You may have to mail in your deposits. If you are interested in an online bank, be sure it is insured by the FDIC.

Check Yourself

1. When is the amount of a purchase you make with a debit card subtracted from your account?

2. List five questions you would ask before opening a checking account.

    a.

    b.

    c.

    d.

    e.

3. What two things should you do with your monthly bank statement?

    a.

    b.

www.walch.com

4. List six good features to look for in a checking account.

   a.

   b.

   c.

   d.

   e.

   f.

5. Why shouldn't you put your Social Security number on your checks?

6. What is the purpose of the checkbook ledger that goes with your checks?

Continued ➤

7. What information is on your monthly bank statement?

8. Why should you never sign a blank check?

9. If you write a check for $30, where should you write the number 3 on the line?

10. How should you keep track of purchases made with a debit card?

11. What are three ways to use an ATM safely?

    a.

    b.

    c.

A Savings Account

There are many places to save money: in a piggy bank, under a mattress, buried in the garden, or in a book. A savings account is a better choice. Your money will not be lost, stolen, or thrown out if it's in the bank.

Best of all, the bank pays you interest on the money in your account. This helps your money grow faster.

When you make a deposit into your account, you must fill out a deposit slip. To take money out of the account, you complete a withdrawal slip.

You may have a passbook savings account. Or, you may get a monthly statement of your account in the mail. Either the passbook or the statement will show your deposits and withdrawals, plus the balance (the total amount in your account).

DEPOSIT TICKET

WILLIAM H. JOHNSON

Date _____

Standard Bank

1234 5678 9123 4567

NET DEPOSIT $

There are many types of savings accounts. Here is a description of three basic types of accounts.

1. **A regular savings account**

   This is the most common type of account for beginning savers. You can open a regular savings account with a small amount of money. (The exact amount will depend on your bank. It could be as little as $25.) You can withdraw (take out) money from the account at any time you want.

2. **A money market account**

   A money market account is an account that pays more interest than a regular savings account. Usually a high amount of money is needed to open a money market account. You will probably have to agree to leave a minimum amount of money in the account at all times.

3. **Certificates of deposit (CDs)**

   CDs are another way to save money. If you put money in a CD, you agree to leave it there for a certain period of time. Usually CDs are for periods from six months to five years. A CD pays more interest than a regular savings account. But if you need the money before the time is up, you will pay a penalty (an extra charge).

Each bank has its own types of savings accounts. One bank may have an account that fits your needs better than another bank. Ask a bank officer to explain the different types of savings accounts that bank offers. Then decide which type meets your needs.

TYPE OF SAVINGS		RATE OF INTEREST
PASSBOOK SAVINGS		2.5 %
MONEY MARKET ACCOUNT		3.625 %
CDs	6 MONTHS	4.25 %
	12 MONTHS	4.50 %
	5 YEARS	5.125 %

www.walch.com

Credit Cards

With a credit card, you can charge your payment instead of using cash for the things you buy. Department stores and gas stations often have their own credit cards. Major credit cards can be used in many places. Some major credit card companies are VISA, Discover, American Express, and MasterCard.

Credit cards are good for emergencies. For example, if your heater stops working in December and you're out of money, you can charge the purchase of a new one. If your car breaks down far from home, your credit card can help you get and pay for repairs on the spot.

Each month you'll get a statement that tells how much you have charged on your credit card. Be sure to pay off the balance each month. That way, you won't run up a large bill you can't pay off. Also, you won't have to pay interest charges.

If you don't pay the full amount, you will be charged interest. Interest is a fee you pay to the credit card company if you pay less than you owe. If you pay less than you owe, you will find yourself getting into debt.

When you get your monthly statement, check it over carefully. Make sure all the charges are correct. You can also check how many charges you've made during the month online or by calling the customer service number.

Credit cards can be helpful in managing your money. But it's too easy to get carried away when you pay with a credit card instead of cash. Credit cards must be used with care.

Credit is not more money. Credit is a way to buy now and pay later. "Pay later" may come sooner than you think! Credit isn't free. You pay to borrow money.

Overuse of credit can be dangerous to your wealth. Credit can be addictive.

Before you pay with a credit card, remember:

- Using a credit card is like taking out a loan. You must pay back what you borrow plus interest of up to 20% or more.

- It's easy to get into trouble using a lot of credit cards. One is enough!

- Keep track of how much you've charged. Try to pay it off each month.

Using a Credit Card

Your bank may help you get a major credit card. These can be used in many different places. Also, some stores issue store credit cards. These can be used only at that store.

Here are some good and bad points about credit cards.

Good Points

- Credit cards can give you a source of money for unexpected or emergency expenses.

- Using a credit card is safer than carrying a large amount of cash.

- You may need a credit card to get airline tickets, hotel rooms, or rental cars.

- If you use your card correctly, it can help you build a good credit rating.

- If your card is lost or stolen, report it to the credit card company right away. Then you will not be responsible for charges over $50 that you did not make yourself.

Bad Points

- Sometimes people buy too much with their credit cards. If you use your card to buy more than you can afford, you will go into debt.

- If you pay the bill late or miss a payment, you will be charged a fee.

- If you don't pay the balance on the card each month, you will be charged interest.

I don't think I'll ever be able to pay this off.

How to Choose a Credit Card

- Get the lowest interest rate you can find.

- Look for a card with no annual fee (or a low annual fee).

- Read the terms of the credit card. Find out about late fees, cash advance fees, annual fees, and other fees.

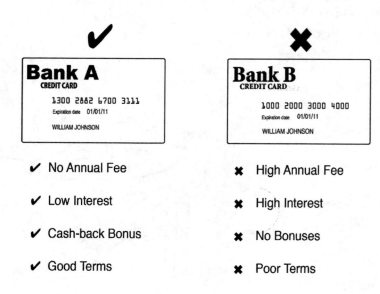

✔

Bank A
CREDIT CARD
1300 2882 6700 3111
Expiration date 01/01/11
WILLIAM JOHNSON

✔ No Annual Fee

✔ Low Interest

✔ Cash-back Bonus

✔ Good Terms

✖

Bank B
CREDIT CARD
1000 2000 3000 4000
Expiration date 01/01/11
WILLIAM JOHNSON

✖ High Annual Fee

✖ High Interest

✖ No Bonuses

✖ Poor Terms

A Bank Loan

Sometimes people get a loan from the bank to buy a car, furniture, or another big-ticket item. Before you get a loan, think it through. If you really need the item, fine. Try not to go into debt for something you don't really need or something that won't last as long as the payments will!

If you need to get a bank loan, shop around. Check at the bank, the credit union, and the place where you're purchasing the item. Get the loan at the place that charges the least interest. You'll save money!

Sometimes lenders try to push longer-term loans with lower payments. A seven-year car loan will have lower monthly payments than a five-year loan or a three-year loan. But you will be paying far more in total interest for the seven-year loan. In the end, the car will cost you far more because you'll be paying for it for several more years. Be careful if a lender tries to sell you a longer-term loan.

Don't sign any papers until you understand the terms of the loan. Don't be afraid to ask questions. Think it through before you sign.

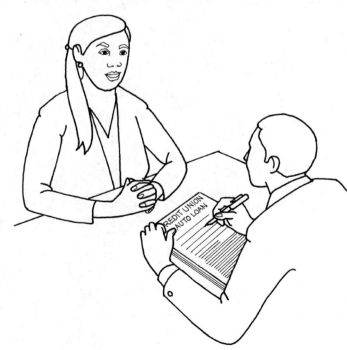

By making a bigger down payment, you'll pay interest on a smaller amount of money.

Pay off the loan as soon as you can.

Keeping Your Personal Information Safe

Thieves are always on the lookout for people's personal information. If they get ahold of your Social Security number, birth certificate, or credit card number, they can steal your identity. They can get credit cards in your name. Then whatever they buy is charged to you!

Here are some ways to help keep your personal information safe:

- Lock up your Social Security card, birth certificate, passport, and other important identification papers.

- Shred bills, bank statements, and credit card statements. Never just toss them in the trash. You can buy an inexpensive shredder for less than $30.

- Don't give out personal information on the phone unless you made the call.

- Make a copy of credit cards and identification you carry in your wallet. Copy front and back. This way you will have information you need in case these items are lost or stolen.

- Don't carry more credit or debit cards than you really need.

- Memorize your PIN (personal identification number). Never write it on the card. Never carry it in your wallet with the card.

- Report lost or stolen cards immediately.

- Request a free copy of your credit report once a year. Order free reports online at www.annualcreditreport.com. (Avoid other Web sites that charge you for this same information.)

- When you order checks, don't have your Social Security number or driver's license number printed on the checks.

- When you order new checks, pick them up at the bank instead of having them mailed.

- If you go on vacation, have the post office hold your mail. Don't let it pile up.

Check Yourself

1. Name two reasons to save your money in a savings account rather than at home.

    a.

    b.

2. What do you fill out when you put money in your savings account?

3. What do you fill out to take money out of your savings account?

4. Which type of savings account can be opened with a small amount of money?

5. Why do you think a CD pays more interest than a regular savings account?

6. What will happen if you take your money out of a CD before the time is up?

7. How could you decide which type of savings account is best for you?

8. Why do you think it is easy to get in trouble if you have several credit cards?

9. What is the difference between a major credit card and a store credit card?

10. Name two wise uses of credit cards.

    a.

    b.

11. Give two reasons why you need to pay off the balance on your credit card each month.

    a.

    b.

12. How do you know how much you have charged on your credit card during the month?

Continued ➤

13. What are two good features to look for when choosing a credit card?

    a.

    b.

14. Where could you go if you were shopping around for a bank loan?

15. Why should you never sign loan papers unless you understand everything they say?

www.walch.com

16. Where should you keep your original Social Security card and birth certificate?

17. Why should you never throw credit card or bank statements in the trash?

18. Why should you make a copy of the cards you carry in your wallet?

19. What should you do if a person calls and says he's from the bank? He says he needs your bank account number to make sure there are no problems with your account.

20. Where could you get a copy of your credit report at no charge?

21. If your credit card is lost or stolen, what should you do?

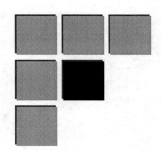

PART 3

Being a Wise Consumer

Be a Careful Shopper

Think Before You Buy

Before you make a purchase, stop and think. Do you really need this item? If you need something and have the money, buy it. If you don't really need it, think it through before you decide whether to buy. Spending only $10 a week on things you can do without will cost you $520 in a year! Ask yourself these questions:

- "What are my goals?"

- "Will this help me reach them?"

Get the Most for Your Money

If you decide to buy, get the most for your money. Know what you're buying. Talk to other people who own the product. Read a consumer buying guide. Look at different models of the item. Test out or study the item. Make sure it's of good quality.

Read the warranty. It tells you the standards the item must meet.

Read the tag or label carefully. It will give you a lot of information about the product.

If you can, wait and buy things on sale. Compare prices at different stores. Doing your homework can save you a lot of money!

Comparison Shopping Is the Key

The key to wise buying is comparison shopping. Of course, you'd like to pay less for what you buy. But this does not mean the cheapest product is always the best one to buy.

When you shop, compare prices, of course. But also ask yourself these questions:

- How well is it made?

- How long will it last?

- How easy will it be to take care of?

Be careful. The less expensive product may not last as long. It may not look good. On the other hand, you may not be able to tell the difference!

Be smart. Buy what you really need, even if it costs a little more. But don't buy more than you need, either.

This coat costs $10 more, but it looks like it's much better made. It will last longer, so it's worth the extra money.

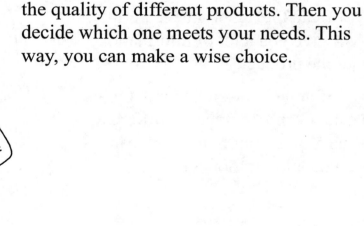

This is what comparison shopping is all about. You compare the price and the quality of different products. Then you decide which one meets your needs. This way, you can make a wise choice.

Think Before You Buy

Have you ever bought something and wondered why you bought it a week later? Being aware of why you make a purchase may help you save money.

Here are some things to think about:

- Some people shop because they're bored. Shopping can be a lot of fun. Choosing nice things and bringing them home may make you feel good. Find something else to do with your time, and you'll avoid coming home with unwanted items!

- Some people buy things on impulse. Stores know how to make attractive displays of goods. And they put them right where you'll be sure to see them. Shop with a list and you'll be less likely to throw extras into the cart.

What should we do?   Let's go shopping.

www.walch.com

- Some people will buy something just because it's on sale. Buying something that you need on sale is good shopping. But a good price is no bargain if the item is something you don't need. You may end up spending a lot on sale items you don't really want or need.

- Some people shop when they're under stress. They say buying things makes them feel better. That may be true for a minute. But when it's time to pay the bill, it may be a different story!

- Some people buy because they think they'll be happier, more attractive, or more interesting if they have this item. This is often what ads (and some sales persons) try to get you to think. Think for yourself! You will be the same person with or without that purchase!

- Some people go out to eat all the time. Going out to eat for one or more meals a day adds up fast. Just grabbing coffee or a soft drink adds up, too. Think of ways to spend time with friends that don't involve going out for food or drinks.

Where to Buy

Let's say you have decided to go ahead with a big purchase. You need this item. And you've saved up the money.

You've also done some homework. First, you read about the item in a consumer magazine or on a Web site. Then you looked at your friends' models. You have a good idea of what you want. But where should you go to buy it?

You may want to start by going to a large store that carries a number of models. That way, you can compare and see what model you would like.

By doing this, you may narrow your choices down to one or two. Next, go home and shop by phone. Call several stores and get their price on the item you want. You may find that prices on the same item vary widely.

Don't forget to check your local newspaper ads. You may find just what you want on sale.

Catalogs, catalog stores, online stores, and discount stores are other places to check.

When you find the best price, buy from that store. But be sure the store has a reputation for standing behind the things it sells before you buy.

The computer program I need costs $49.95 at Great Buy. But it's on sale at Computer Corral for $39.95. I guess I'll go to Computer Corral.

When to Buy

The same item does not always sell for the same price. Look for sales. Many sales can save you money.

You can count on certain things being on sale at certain times of the year. Many things are marked down after Christmas. White sales (towels, sheets, and linens) come in January.

You can find good buys at end-of-season sales, too. By August, most shorts, swimsuits, and other summer clothes are marked way down. Garden tools, lawn mowers, and outdoor furniture are on sale, too. Stores don't have space to keep all these things stored until the next year, so they move them out at sale prices.

Rebate offers and coupons can save you money, too. You save even more if you can use your coupon on something that's also on sale. Just be sure it's something you really want.

Most sales offer you a chance to save money—but watch out. Some "sales" are not really sales. Be sure that prices are really marked down. If the original price is high, the sale price may still not be a good deal!

Saving Money at the Grocery Store or Drug Store

You can get more for your money at the grocery store or drug store. It's not hard at all. It only requires a little time in advance.

Here are some easy money-saving ideas:

- Use a shopping list. Keep a pad and pencil in the kitchen. Write down items as you use them up. This helps you be ready to get everything you need at one time.

- Look at the newspapers and ads for sales and coupons. Most grocery stores and drug stores run weekly ads. You can save by getting the things you need when they are on sale.

- Clip coupons for items you normally buy or would like to try. You can find coupons in the newspaper or online. Organize the coupons so you can easily find coupons for things you plan to buy that week.

- If you can use a coupon on an item that's on sale, you'll save more!

- Some stores double coupons. If a coupon is marked $.50, the store will double it for a savings of $1.00. If the store also has a sale on an item you have a coupon for, you may get a really good price!

- You don't always save money with coupons. Another brand may be on sale that week. Or it may be cheaper than the price of the first item even with the coupon. Check to be sure.

- Make sure you don't shop on an empty stomach! If you are hungry when you shop for food, you are more likely to buy extras you don't need.

- Buy extra of items you use a lot when they're on sale. But be careful not to buy more than you can use.

- Try store brands. The store-brand aspirin may contain the same ingredients and be far cheaper (even if you have a coupon for the name brand).

- When you are ready to check out with your purchases, keep your eyes on the scanner! Often items ring up at the wrong price. The computer may not be giving you the sale price that is advertised. Watch carefully or you may not get the bargains you went in the store to find.

Be Advised

Ads are everywhere! Each ad hopes to sell you something. You can learn a lot from ads. You may find out about a new product. You learn about special sales. But think for yourself. Don't accept everything an ad says. Remember, the goal of each ad is to get you to buy.

Read the ads below. Circle the letter of the correct answer(s) to each question. For some questions, you should circle more than one answer.

1. In this ad you are not given:

    a. the price of Healthy Kid Drink

    b. the ingredients of Healthy Kid Drink

    c. the size of the container

2. This ad tries to convince you that the car:

    a. will be easy to pay for

    b. will make you popular

    c. gets great gas mileage

Continued ➡

3. This ad says that the 13-inch color TV:

   a. costs $298

   b. is on sale Friday and Saturday only

   c. will be delivered free

4. After reading this ad, you know for sure that:

   a. the computers are a good buy

   b. the store has easy terms

   c. the computers are sold by Mac's Computers

5. This ad says that:

   a. all jogging suits are 40% off

   b. jogging suits are on sale for different amounts up to 40% off

   c. jogging suits are $40 off the original price

Read the Warranty

A warranty or guarantee tells you that a product is of a certain quality. For example, stereo speakers may be guaranteed to work for one year. Read the warranty carefully. Know your rights!

When you buy a big item, keep the receipt and the warranty or guarantee. This way, if the product does not work, you can get it replaced or repaired. Often, you can take the item back to the store where you got it. Sometimes you must mail it to the manufacturer.

Look at the warranty below. Then use it to answer the questions on the next page.

WARRANTY—ONE-YEAR GUARANTEE

Easy-Play will replace without charge (except for labor) any part that proves defective within 1 year of purchase date. No labor charge within 90 days of purchase. This guarantee applies only to the original owner. It does not apply to damage resulting from accidents, neglect, or abuse. The TV must be returned to the Easy-Play dealer where purchased.

On each line, write the letter(s) that show what expenses you would pay for each TV needing repair.

a. parts   **b.** labor   **c.** parts & labor   **d.** nothing

You would pay for:

1. A TV that breaks 30 days after purchase _____

2. A TV that breaks 4 months after purchase _____

3. A TV you bought used _____

4. A TV that was dropped _____

Complain, Complain!

Have you ever had this happen? You buy a product, and it falls apart when you get it home. You buy something, and it doesn't work. You buy food, and it's spoiled when you open the package. What can you do? What rights do you have?

A Simple Return

If an item you buy doesn't fit or is missing a part, you may be able to just return it to the store. Some stores will not give a refund without your receipt. Other stores require that you return the item within a certain number of days. Some stores will not give you a refund. Instead, they give you store credit.

It's a good idea to know the return policy of stores where you shop. That way you'll be able to follow their directions and get your money back! If the store is not helpful with the return, you may want to think twice before shopping there again!

A Problem Return

It's a good idea to keep receipts, the warranty, and instructions for your purchases. For example, if you buy a camera, keep the receipt, the warranty, and the instructions. Have a file in which you keep this information for everything major you buy. Then if there's a problem, you'll be prepared.

Let's say you buy a camera and it stops working after three months. You look in your file and see that the camera has a one-year warranty. Go to the store with your camera and the paperwork. Explain the problem. They may replace the camera right then.

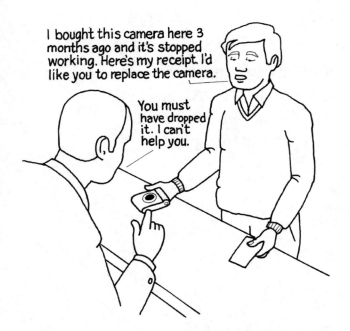

If the store is not helpful, you may have to write a letter to the company that made the camera. Or you may find a customer service number on your paperwork. Either way, tell what the problem is. Be sure you are polite. Explain what you want them to do. If they want to see your receipt, send a copy, not the original. Keep a record of who you talked to and what was done. If you keep at it, you'll get what you want.

In rare cases, nothing will work. If this happens, try contacting:

- the consumer action line of your local newspaper
- the Better Business Bureau

Check Yourself

1. What are some questions to ask yourself before you buy?

2. Where can you get information about a pricey item you are thinking about buying?

3. When you comparison shop, what two things do you check about the different products you look at?

   a.

   b.

4. When might the product with the lowest price not be the best one to buy?

5. You are shopping for a mountain bike. Name four things you could do to comparison shop before you buy.

   a.

   b.

   c.

   d.

6. When might a sale price not really be a good price?

7. When would be the best time of year to save money on:
   a. linens/towels?

   b. summer clothes?

   c. winter clothes?

   d. a lawn mower?

Continued ▶

www.walch.com

8. How can ads be helpful to the consumer?

9. How can ads get you to buy things you don't need?

10. You buy an item that doesn't work. How can you prove to the store the date you bought it?

11. What should you do in each of these cases?

    a. You buy milk. When you open it at home, it's sour.

    b. You buy a camera. The camera won't take a picture.

    c. You buy a radio. It doesn't work. But the store won't take it back.

www.walch.com

Your Weekly Shopping

How much do you spend per month on food? How much do you spend on non-food items such as toothpaste, aspirin, shampoo, and so on?

Try adding it up for a month to find out. You may be surprised! For most people, food and basic non-food items add up to a lot of money!

You can save by planning ahead. Here are some ways that you can plan ahead:

Read the Ads

Before you go to the store, read the newspaper ads. Plan what you're going to eat that week around the foods that are on sale.

Make a List

Making a list can save you time and money! During the week, write down things as you run out of them. Before you go to the store, plan your meals. List what you'll need to fix those meals. You'll spend less if you make only one trip a week to the store than if you go every day.

Use Coupons

Coupons can save you money. Using coupons on sale items saves you double! But use them only on things you need.

Try Store Brands

See page 72 for more about this.

Check the Unit Price

See page 73.

Be on Guard at the Checkout

When the checker rings up your purchases, watch for mistakes. You may not get the sale price on a sale item. Tell the checker if there is a mistake.

Brand Name or Store Brand?

On a brand-name product, the company that makes it puts its "brand" on the product. Then the product is heavily advertised. The company hopes that you will try the product. Then, if you like it, you will look for that brand again.

Many large stores also carry "store-brand" products. These products usually have a lower price than the brand-name products. That's because they are not widely advertised.

Which is better to buy: a brand name or a store brand? The brand name often costs more, but the quality is usually good. And you may have a coupon for it.

The store brand is often just as good in terms of quality. In fact, it may even be made by the brand-name company! A good idea is to try the store brands at your favorite grocery store. If you like them, you'll save money. If you don't like an item, then switch to the name brand with the higher price.

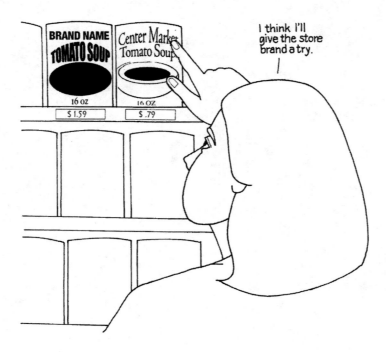

Unit Pricing

At the grocery or drug store, you may see several sizes of a product. How do you know which is the best buy?

Look at the unit pricing tags on the shelves. The unit price tells the cost per ounce or the cost per item. A lower unit price is the better buy.

The unit price tag helps you get the best deal without having to do the math. The unit price is the real price of that item.

But don't just look at the price. You won't save money if you buy more than you can use before the food spoils. You won't save, either, if you don't like what you buy and don't use it. Sometimes it's worth more money to get a ready-made food, instead of something you must fix from scratch.

Look at the unit price tags for the peanuts in the picture. Answer the questions.

$1.92
unit price is $ .12 / ounce

$1.92
unit price is $ .06 / ounce

1. Which container gives you the most peanuts?

2. Which container of peanuts has a lower unit price?

3. What do you notice about these two containers of peanuts?

www.walch.com

Check Yourself

1. Why do you think you'll spend less per week with one big weekly grocery trip than if you go to the grocery store every day?

2. How do you think you could save coupons so they would be easier for you to use?

3. When do you think that using a coupon would not save you money?

4. When could a brand-name food be a better buy than the store brand?

5. What do you think are some good reasons for trying store-brand products?

6. Why do you think someone might not buy a store-brand product even though it is lower priced?

7. Give two examples of times when the product with the lower unit price would not be a good buy.

   a.

   b.

8. How could you save money by reading the grocery ads?

9. Why is it a good idea to keep a list of items you have run out of during the week?

10. What information can you find on the unit pricing tag?

Words to Know

annual fee	yearly amount charged to use a credit card
ATM	automated teller machine; a machine into which you can insert your ATM card and withdraw money from your account
balance	amount of money in a checking or savings account, or money still to be paid on a loan
basic needs	things needed to live: food, shelter, clothing, etc.
bounced check	a check that must be returned to the bank because there is not enough money in the account to cover it; a returned check
brand name	a product labeled with the name given to it by the company that made it, such as Crest® or Tide®
certificate of deposit (CD)	a time deposit that pays higher interest than a savings account but has a penalty for early withdrawal of funds
comparison shopping	comparing price and quality before buying
consumer	a person who buys or uses goods or services
credit	a way to buy now and pay later
credit card	a card that lets you buy on credit
credit report	a report listing your debts, activity on your accounts, and credit rating
credit union	a non-profit organization that offers financial services
debit card	a card that looks like a credit card, but causes the amount of the purchase to be subtracted right away from your checking or savings account

deductions	amounts taken out of the paycheck
deposit	an amount put into an account
down payment	a part of the full price paid at the time of purchase
end-of-season sale	a sale on items that will soon be out-of-season
FDIC	Federal Deposit Insurance Corporation—a government agency that insures bank accounts
FICA	a paycheck deduction that is held for Social Security
goals	something you want to work toward
gross pay	the amount of money earned, before deductions
guarantee	warranty (see next page)
identity theft	stealing of your peronal information to commit crimes
impulse buying	buying something without thinking it through
interest	money paid for the use of money lent
late fee	charge for paying your bill late
ledger	a chart for keeping track of how much money is in a bank account
money market account	a bank account that earns interest and restricts the type and number of withdrawals
net pay	"take-home" pay; what is left of your paycheck after deductions have been taken out
online bank	a bank that exists only on the Internet; a virtual bank
online banking	the ability to access your account and pay bills online

online bill pay	a system that allows you to pay your bills on the bank's Web site
PIN	personal identification number; needed for some transactions
rebate	a return of part of a payment
receipt	a slip of paper telling the amount paid and the date
regular savings account	an account with a low minimum balance and a lower rate of interest
return policy	store rules for returning items purchased
statement	a record of deposits, withdrawals, and the balance in your account
store brand	a product labeled with a store's private label, or name
unit pricing	cost per ounce or cost per unit
utilities	services such as electricity, gas, phone, and water/sewer
warranty	guarantee; a promise that a product is of good quality and that the maker will fix any defects within a certain time period after purchase
white sale	a sale on sheets, towels, and related items
withdrawal	taking money out of an account